FAYGALA
Yiddish Refugee

Betty Baker with
Irene McKinney, PhD

Based on a true story

OlivePress
צהר זית

Messianic & Christian Publisher

FAYGALA Yiddish Refugee

Details were added to the story by Olive Press Publisher (with written permission from the family). Thus it has to be called fiction.

Printed in the USA
ISBN 978-0-9790873-9-4
1. Jewish Fiction 2. Historical Fiction 3. Educational Fiction

Cover and interior pencil drawings:
Copyright © 2014
by Artist, Karen Van Lieu, kavanlieu@gmail.com

Karen A. Van Lieu

Turin, NY 13473

Cover design, photos on back cover, pages 8, 18 copyright © 2015
by Cheryl Zehr, Olive Press Publisher
Photo page 34 from Microsoft Office clipart online.
All other photos are copyright free from the Library of Congress.

Published by

Olive Press
צהר | זית

Messianic & Christian Publisher

www.olivepresspublisher.org
olivepressbooks@gmail.com

This book is dedicated to Faygala and all Jewish people over the centuries who courageously did what had to be done to survive, to carry on their traditions, and to pass down their faith.

TABLE OF CONTENTS

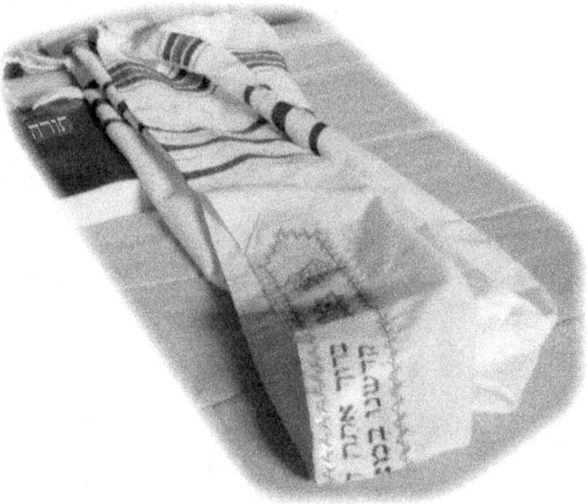
תורה

THE VILLAGE

F aygala peeked through the lattice separating the women from the men in the *shul*, the meeting place. At nearly seventeen, Faygala still loved watching the men reverently unfold their prayer *talliths* and begin reciting the blessing over them.

"Baruch ata ADONAI Elohenu ... Blessed are you LORD our God ...." All the men from age 13 to elderly were standing in a circle, each looking at the beautiful border of their tallith where the blessing is lovingly embroidered by their wife or mother. Faygala watched as they finished reciting the blessing, kissed the ends of the border, then flipped the flowing, blue and white cloths over their backs. They held them over their heads for a silent, prayerful moment before wrapping them around their shoulders.

Faygala especially kept her eye on Yitz'khak who was standing beside her older brother, Feivel. She admired the great reverence with which Yitz'khak handled his tallith and performed this sacred ceremony.

There were fourteen men today. Faygala could remember when the shul hall was full of men and boys. Now it was nearly empty. Still, there were enough to make the ten men needed for a minyan. So there would be a Shabbos service today. If the minyan was not complete, no service could be held. Everyone would have to go home.

Faygala's people were Jewish. They lived in Russia and spoke Yiddish. They said *Shabbos* for Shabbat or Sabbath; *shul* for synagogue; *Bubbie* for Grandma; *kuzineh* for cousin; *shtetle* for village; *shtetlach* for villages, etc.

The concern in their small *shetl* was how soon the day would come when there would no longer be ten men for a minyan. Every year more families left to protect their fathers and sons from being conscripted by the dreaded army. Now there were only two rabbis and one cantor left in the shul. Yitz'khak's father, the head rabbi, was still here along with Yitz'khak and his three younger brothers. Rabbi David was still here, but all his sons were gone already to America.

"Ma toh vu ..." Now they were singing about how beautiful Jacob's tents are. Faygala loved this tune. It always brought warmth to her heart. The rhythm felt like being rocked in Bubbie's rocking chair.

"Shema Yisrial ADONAI Elohenu ... Hear O Israel the LORD our God ...." The cantor's deep voice rang out. The women always stood for the Shema part of the service. Faygala wanted to sing out mightily with all her heart, but she didn't. She sang quietly like a proper Jewish girl, along with all the other proper Jewish women and girls around her. They were supposed to sing quietly enough so the men couldn't hear them. The men's voices usually rang out so strongly that they drowned out the women's singing, but that was getting harder and harder as the number of men was dwindling faster than the number of women.

"... ADONAI echad. Baruch shem kavod malchuto, le olam vaed ...the LORD is one. Blessed be the name of His glorious kingdom forever more." The Shema continued. Faygala listened. She thought she could hear Yitz'khak's voice ringing out above the others. She leaned her head and peeked over the lattice. Just then he turned his head and their eyes met. Faygala quickly drew back and pulled her scarf up over her head acting like she was cold. She didn't want Mama or her Bubbies to notice her cheeks turning red.

"Ve ahavta et ADONAI Elolecha ...And you shall love the LORD your God...." The cantor's lone, chanting voice now rang out and filled the whole shul with its beauty and reverence. "... u b'kol levevlekha ... and with all your heart ...." Faygala closed her eyes and tried to imagine that it was Papa's strong voice ringing forth instead of Cantor Yishai's. She did this every Shabbos. She didn't want to forget what Papa's voice sounded like. Cantor Yishai's voice was wonderful, but Papa's was far better— to Faygala anyway. "... and upon your gates."

As everyone sat, Faygala squeezed in between her two Bubbies, ready to relax and enjoy their quiet attention on her while the men carried on with their long Torah service. Faygala felt blessed to have two grandmas. Most of her friends in Naganovitzki Shtetl didn't have any. Actually, one of her Bubbies, Bubbie Etkie, wasn't her real grandma. She was her real Bubbie's sister, Mama's Aunt Etkie, and Cousin Khannah's mother. Mama's mother had passed away long before Faygala was born when Mama was still young.

At family gatherings, Bubbie Etkie would say, "Faygala, have another *shtickel* ... piece ... of *Khallah*, you are too thin."

Bubbie Malkie would say. "Put some *kreplach* in your chicken soup, you need the strength."

Whenever Bubbie Etkie saw Faygala passing by her house, she would call out, "Faygala, come in. I made some potato *latkes*. You'll come have a taste, won't you?" Faygala never refused. She loved the pampering she received in that home from Bubbie Etkie and from Cousin Khannah.

Kuzineh Khannah taught Faygala how to fix her hair pretty. She crocheted a lacy collar for Faygala's Shabbat dress and embroidered a fancy pillow case especially for Faygala's bed while teaching her how to crochet and embroider, too.

Kuzineh Khannah and Mama were cousins, but they had grown up like sisters. Faygala remembers Kuzineh Khannah coming over many times to help Mama with household chores. Sometimes Mama went to their house to help Kuzineh Khannah and Bubbie Etkie with shelling peas, snipping beans, husking corn, canning, and quilting. Feivel and Faygala were always required to join in the work while their little brother, Mendeleh, was allowed to run around their chairs playing games with the peapods or corncobs. Feivel soon grew too old for women's work.

He then helped Papa and the shtetl men with the animal and field work. After Papa left for America, the men in turn helped Feivel keep the farm going for Mama.

For many years now, there has been no Kuzineh Khannah at Bubbie Etkie's house. Faygala could still remember the wedding. What a happy day it was! The bride and groom looked so enraptured standing under the *khupah*. They had used the groom's father, Rabbi David's tallith for the khupah canopy. The groom, Rabbi David's youngest son, Yankel, wore his new tallit, hand embroidered by Kuzineh Khannah.

Faygala jumped when the Yankel broke the wine glass. Then, oh how the men danced and hollered with joy as they carried the groom around, high above their heads in his special chair! But everything changed when the laughter gave way to tearful good-by hugs as Kuzineh Khannah's new husband took her away in the buggy, leaving for America.

That was so long ago that Faygala couldn't even remember what Kuzineh Khannah looked like anymore. Mama often said to Faygala, "Don't worry, Faygala, someday you will go live with my kuzineh in America. Then you will see again what she looks like. I'm sure you will recognize her as soon as you lay your eyes on her."

Faygala glanced over at Mama just now in the shul. She was wearing her special, Shabbos shawl, reading silently from her *Siddur* prayer book. Faygala's little brother, Mendeleh, was leaning against her arm. Papa bought the shawl for Mama one time when he had to go to the city. That was many years ago before all the trouble began. The shawl still looked as good as new because Mama only wore it to shul and took special care of it.

A couple years after Kuzineh Khannah's wedding, the wrenching day came when dear Papa left for America. Faygala didn't like to talk about, or even think about, that day. It hurt too much. But she did like to think about Papa. She could still hear her Papa's strong voice saying his Hebrew prayers three times a day: every morning, afternoon, and night. Sometimes she lay in bed pretending he was telling her another story. She forced herself to remember every word of the ones he had told her over the years, some from the Jewish Scriptures, some from Jewish history, and some that he made up. Many times, lately, little Mendeleh has been climbing up the ladder to Faygala's bed and begging her to tell him a story. She always began, "Papa once told me this story about....."

Papa's stories were what helped keep Faygala's budding faith alive. Like a tree planted firmly in the ground, the rigid faith of all the Jews living in Naganovitzki had deep roots that sustained them in their unwavering observance of the traditions and rituals of Judaism and Yiddishkeit. For centuries, Jewish people had lived in shtetlach like Naganovitzki in Russia and Eastern Europe under regimes that imposed harsh restrictions upon them. In 1904, things were only getting worse. Jewish people were now not even being allowed to own property or do business. They were being denied almost all the rights of citizenship and were kept in degradation, poverty, and fear. Even their women could no longer walk about safely.

Ironically, those in power whose hatred wanted to drive all Jews into their graves were thwarted by those already buried. Stories of ancestors' faithfulness, perseverance, and bravery not only enriched the Jewish culture, but also gave purpose to this way of life. The love and strength of family and faith in God enabled Jewish people to survive in this hostile land of unbearable oppression.

The more adventurous men and women left the teetering "safety" of the known for what seemed the riskier unknown: emigrating to the "golden land of America." The letters they sent back home spoke glowingly of freedom and a chance for a better life. Mothers and grandmothers got used to seeing their loved ones leave, not knowing whether they would ever see them again.

Children, however, could not get used to such a thing. Faygala would never get used to having her papa gone. She thought of him every day. She cherished his letters. She watched for the mail wagon every morning, hoping for another one. She always sent a loving letter back, along with Mama's long one. Their envelope was always stuffed thick. Mama spent many a late night writing to Papa. His replies took months to arrive, but every word seemed fresh to Faygala.

The shul service was now coming to a close. The women stood for the priestly blessing. Faygala leaned over the lattice again to gaze at the sea of white as each man pulled their talliths over their heads for this blessing. The fathers of young boys held theirs out like wings and their sons gathered under them to receive the blessing. When Faygala was little, she used to slip down the stairs at this time and run to Papa to huddle under his tallith with Feivel. Papa always winked at her and held out his tallith over her as he chanted the blessing for the congregation. Faygala noticed a couple little girls doing the same right now—finding shelter under their Papas' tallith "wings."

In all her sixteen years, Faygala had never spent a night away from her mother or her two brothers. Living in Russia in her little shtetl was like living on an island in the middle of an ocean of hostility. Even their Yiddish language was different. The people outside spoke Russian. Most of the villagers didn't even know Russian.

The adults in the shtetl protected the children in every way possible, even their tender, little ears from hearing anything from the outside world—the increasing unrest between the Cossacks and the Russian army, called the Bolsheviks, or the persecution and pogroms growing ever more intense all around the country. They hushed such conversations when the children came near.

As a protective older brother, Feivel kept a watchful eye on his blossoming teenage sister, but Mama still feared for her. "Faygala *ziskeit* ... sweetheart, be careful and don't walk alone anywhere. You are a *shaina maidel* ... such a pretty girl, with your long brown hair and brown eyes." To further insure Faygala's safety, her mother broke the protective silence and began to tell her stories about young Jewish girls who were "misused" by the Cossack soldiers, and she said to be careful not to catch the eye of the noblemen or Russian soldiers, either. She thought this would scare Faygala into being careful. But it didn't work.

The River

One unusually warm, early spring day, again Faygala couldn't resist running down to the river behind her house. So, when Mama wasn't looking, she snuck out. If she didn't stay away too long, Mama wouldn't even know. She felt she just *had* to walk along the riverbank and breathe in the freshness of the breeze wafting across the water. A few wild flowers and new grass leaves were just beginning to peek through the dry, tall grasses still brown from last fall, while noisy blackbirds were laying claim to their territories. She could almost taste the sweet smell of sprouting clover in the yonder fields. She lifted her arms up to the sky and danced along the wet shore. Feeling too warm, she took off her heavy shoes—her only pair of shoes—and her long brown cotton stockings. She thrilled at the feel of the cool, damp earth to her feet.

Then she sat on a rock ledge and dangled her toes in the rushing river, letting her mind get lost in a daydream remembering the last time, a week ago, when she had come down here and encountered Yitz'khak reciting the portion of the *Talmud* he had learned in *Yeshiva* studies that day. She had hoped she would find him here again today. "Oh, he is so handsome. What a tender smile he has, and I like his curly, red beard and his tight side curls."

They had walked together down the village path past this same spot by the river. It seemed like he was headed to the woods up ahead where Eli's Naomi had been snatched and defiled and beaten by a Cossack soldier who had jumped out from behind a tree. Faygala wondered if Yitz'khak really intended to walk with her into the dreaded woods, but she decided if he did, she would go with him because she knew he would protect her. But he didn't. He had stopped before they got to the woods, intent on what he was telling her. They were studying about *Pesakh*, Passover, in the Yeshiva.

"You know that Elohim delivered His people from the Egyptians because He heard their cries. So, today, if He hears our cries of prayer to Him, He may deliver us from the Cossacks. I am crying to Him at the morning, noon, and evening prayers at home and in the shul. Sometimes when I am out here alone, I cry to Him as loud as I can because I want Him to hear us! Perhaps He will even send us the Messiah!" As he talked, Yitz'khak meandered toward the fence beside the road opposite the river and leaned his arms on it. Gazing out at the skipping lambs, he went on explaining what else he had learned in the Torah that day.

The sheep were like pets to everyone in the village. Some of them came over to Yitz'khak for attention. Faygala absentmindedly stepped up on the bottom fence board so she could listen more closely to what Yitz'khak was saying. This brought her up closer to his level. She felt a little nervous being close to a boy and spending so much time with him. They both knew this was forbidden. In their discomfort, they forced their attention to the animals.

They laughed awkwardly together at the playful lambs. Yitz'khak leaned over the fence to pet a ewe. They looked the yearling rams over, discussing which ones would be perfect enough to have been a Pesakh lamb, if the Temple in Jerusalem were still standing today.

"That one there looks really good!" Faygala pointed to the whitest one with the smoothest wool.

"But look at its one ear. There's a scab on it. That would be called a 'blemish.'" Yitz'khak then recited David's beautiful shepherd Psalm to her in Hebrew. She joined him for most of it. Her father had taught it to her long ago—before he left for America. A gray bird landed on a fence post not far from them and began warbling melodically. In response, Yitz'khak sang the Yiddish spring song, "Faygala, Faygala" to the bird and began dancing the Jewish dance step that fit the lively tune.

Faygala's heart warmed, watching his four long *tzit-tzit* fringes fly from under his shirt as he twirled. It brought back memories of watching her father dance at weddings, and on Purim, and even in happy moments at home, coaxing smiles and laughter from Mama. Soon Faygala gleefully joined Yitz'khak. They sang other songs on the riverbank as they danced together—well, not really together. They kept the circle very wide so as to make sure they didn't touch each other. Jewish men and women, young or old, do not dance together.

Exhausted, giggling, and thirsty, they knelt down by the river and slurped up the clear, cold water. As they headed back to the village, Yitz'khak got serious again and, to Faygala's thrilling delight, started talking about their future together. He had wonderful plans for them. He would build them a nice little house. They would have their own sheep and a cow. He would teach in the Yeshiva. He wanted to have lots of children by the time he would take his father's place as leading rabbi of the shul.

Although he was expressing his love for her, Yitz'khak didn't touch her. No Jewish boy is ever allowed to touch a young woman, especially not a young man who was studying in Yeshiva!

As Yitz'khak talked, Faygala gazed at his face, the handsome face of this man who was going to be a rabbi— her rabbi! Her heart swelled with love. "Mama would not like this, I know, because he is only a Yeshiva *bokher* now, but he is in the last year of his studies." He told her he was going to write to her Papa for her hand in marriage very soon. She let out a happy sigh, cherishing their secret in her heart.

Suddenly, coarse shouts and laughter slashed her dreamy thoughts, tearing her away from the sweet memory. Out of the woods came soldiers with their arms around each other in two's and three's, drunkenly singing and staggering down the path. Their disheveled, dirty white tunics were hanging out over their bright red uniform pants.

"Cossacks!!" Snatching her shoes up with her stockings, she darted into the tall grass, trying to stay hidden as she raced away, but the men caught sight of her and ran after her. One of them lunged at her and caught one of her braids, yanking it hard. Her head jerked back, nearly cracking her neck.

"Oh, look what we have here!" He called to the others. "A little Yid girl! Aha, I think she wants to play! Here Sasha, catch her before she gets away." The soldier tossed her to his companion. The whole group started pulling her this way and that, passing her around the circle they had formed, grabbing at her skirt and petticoats, laughing and laughing. She could hardly see for the hot tears streaming down her face. She tried to break free but they were much too strong for her.

Her breath came in short, hard gasps as she cried and pleaded in her limited Russian, "Please, please, let me go. Leave me alone!"

It seemed to go on forever—the coarse laughter—the sweaty, smelly hands—the fierce eyes glaring from their red, puffy faces—their putrid, warm alcohol breath. Suddenly, the chance came when one of the Cossacks stopped for a swig from his bottle. She slipped from his lax grasp and scrambled through the open space in the circle. Running like a frightened gazelle, her ripped skirts trailing behind her, she got away. The men's loud curses followed her, "We'll play again, little Yid girl, next time we see you." She raced at top speed all the way home and collapsed in the doorway, sobbing hysterically.

Her mother lifted her up from the floor. She held the trembling girl against her chest, stroking her hair, rocking and patting her like when she was a little girl. "Shah, shah mein ziskeit ... Shh, shh, my sweetheart." Her mother held her close, singing softly, "Shah, shah mein klaineh Faygala ... Shh, shh, my little Faygala." When the girl stopped crying, her mother led her up the ladder to her bed. "Gut nacht, shlof gezuntahate ... Good night, sleep well," she whispered as she tucked the blankets around her.

Faygala lay crumpled in her bed trying to stop shaking. Every time she fell asleep, her dreams made her relive the whole, frightening event over again. She woke up from each short sleep shuddering at her narrow escape from the filthy Cossacks. She felt so dirty and filthy from their sweaty, rough treatment. She got up, climbed down from her loft and washed herself with the water in the kitchen bucket just below her, using the strong smelling bar of soap. She scrubbed and scrubbed, but couldn't wash the grimy feeling away. Tears streamed down Mama's face as she watched, stroking Faygala's back again.

As she lay back in bed, Faygala began to realize more and more the stark danger of it all. She had barely escaped with her life. Her whole body shivered at the thought. It was so terrifying! Would she ever be able to forget? Would she ever feel safe again?

After Mama put little Mendeleh to bed, she and Feivel talked far into the night. Faygala listened to the low tones of their voices as they tried to figure out what to do for her protection now. Their decisive plans were made by the time they turned in.

For three years Papa had been sending money home from America for them to live on, but also to save for eventually bringing the whole family over. Now, it was important for Faygala to go first and alone.

Papa had told them that passage from the northern seaport, Odessa, to New York City was $34. He wrote that you needed another $25 when you got to Ellis Island to show the immigration officers that you had money and you were not destitute. Feivel figured that another $41 would give Faygala enough money to see her safely there until Papa picked her up at Ellis Island. By HaShem's blessing, their good friend, Pincus, was leaving next week with his family for Odessa to catch a ship for America themselves. He had an old wagon and a couple of horses to take them to the seaport.

That morning, as soon as Feivel said his morning prayers, he went to Pincus' house to see if they could take Faygala with them. Faygala waited in fear and dread.

Feivel returned with the report. "With HaShem's help, we will squeeze her in. That's what Pincus told me," he declared happily to Mama.

"Mama, I don't want to leave you!"

"I know, my child," her mother stroked her hair. "But you must leave. Elohim was watching over you yesterday, Faygala. Believe me, the soldiers will not be so easy with you the next time they catch you."

Faygala persisted, "But Mama, how can you get along without me? You need me to help with the cooking and baking and looking after Mendeleh."

Tears rolled down her mother's cheeks, "Shah, tochter ... be quiet daughter." She cradled Faygala in her arms.

Faygala knew in her heart she had to leave. She had

to leave everything she held so dear: Yitz'khak, Mama, her two brothers and this homey little one-room house. She loved every little bit of her home. She especially loved helping Mama prepare for Shabbos on Friday, giving little Mendeleh his weekly bath, cleaning, and cooking, filling up the house with the wonderful, pleasant smells of freshly baked *khallah*, the special Shabbos bread, and simmering chicken soup. At sundown, Mama covered her head to *bench licht,* light the candles, to welcome the Sabbath. The candles cast their soft glow upon her family bringing in the feeling of rest and reprieve. Shabbos was a day of peace, a relief from the stress of living as a Jew among the Russians.

At the Shabbos meal, in the absence of Papa, Feivel said the blessing over the wine and khallah, and after dinner they all sang *zmirot,* songs. "I hope they keep Shabbos and kosher in Cleveland, Ohio," Faygala included this wish in her prayers that night.

It was a constant struggle to keep a clean house, but Faygala was used to the hard work. Each morning, she swept the dirt floor, and emptied the big pans they used during the night when they didn't want to go to the outhouse. In the summer, Faygala helped Feivel gather rushes to repair the thatched roof. When they were fortunate enough to have a goose for Shabbos dinner, she would pluck the goose's feathers and over the years, her mother had enough soft feathers to make a featherbed, a piranee. She made it for Faygala's marriage bed, but in the meantime she encased it in rough, red flannel, for Faygala to use to keep warm on her sleeping platform above the big, brick oven.

Faygala loved snuggling under the piranee. It kept her toasty warm even when the nights were so cold that ice formed on the water bucket below. She didn't want to leave any of this to go alone to a foreign land.

"Shaina maidel ... Pretty girl, you will like America." Mama continued stroking Faygala's hair. "There you will go to school. You will meet a nice boy. You will get married. Someday you will have a home of your own. You will have a chance for a good life there; here is no good for you.

"Oh Mama! I don't want to meet a nice boy! Yitz'khak is planning to ask Papa for his blessing." Faygala spilled out their secret. "We want to get married. Now, I will never be a *kaleh moid,* a bride because I will never marry anyone else! I don't want to say goodbye to him. I can't bear the thought of never seeing him again. I love him, Mama!" Faygala wailed.

"Little Bird, it breaks my heart to hear you cry. You must be strong. Wipe your tears. Go wash your face. Get dressed. We have things to get ready for your trip. You are leaving on Monday, already. Your Papa and I, we were planning on sending you and Feival to my kuzineh Khannah in America this summer, but we can't wait now."

There was not enough time to do everything that needed to be done or to say everything that needed to be said to all her loved ones. Everybody tried to hold back the tears, but most of them failed.

Faygala kissed Bubbie Malkie and cried, "Will I see you again, Bubbie?"

"Shah, shah my dear child, zol zein shtark ... be strong," Bubbie Malkie held her close and told her to be brave.

"Gay gezunteh hait, go in good health," Bubbie Etkie whispered with tears running down her wrinkled cheeks as she clasped Faygala to her bosom.

Yitz'khak was beside himself with anger and grief. He wanted to take revenge on the soldiers. "I wish I was strong like Samson so I could kill them all with the jaw of a donkey," he told Faygala as they walked down the pathway that led to his family's animal shed.

He was also angry at Faygala for going to the river alone. He scolded her for it, but when he noticed that she was about to cry, his tone changed. "I'm sorry, Faygel. It wasn't your fault. I'm not angry at you. I'm angry at the soldiers." By this time they were out of sight of any watching eyes. Yitz'khak led her behind the barn and turned toward her. "I'm so glad you are still alive and that they didn't hurt you," he said tenderly. Then feeling overwhelmed with gratefulness, he did the forbidden thing for an Orthodox Jewish boy. He pulled her in and held her close. "I don't care if this defiles me," he declared. "It is worth all the cleansing rituals I will have to go through because I might never see you again!" Faygala's heart shrilled as she melted into his loving, safe arms. At this he shed tears. His tears mixed with hers as he leaned his cheek against hers. The thought of an ocean between them was too much to bear.

Yitz'khak pulled away from her and began pacing back and forth as plans began to form in his mind. Soon he began talking very fast as he paced, zitzit sailing in the air at each turn, "I will work hard. I'll do anything for anybody who will pay me. ANYTHING! I'll even feed filthy, nasty, forbidden pigs if I have to. I'll save every penny. I'll figure it out. I'll find a way. Somehow, I will get to America and I will find you."

Faygala watched his tall, lanky form walking to and fro. She loved the look of determination on his face, the clenching of his fists getting ready for the struggle ahead, and the purposeful, firm stepping of his bootclad feet. The more he talked the farther she fell in love with her man— her rabbi. Suddenly she realized what he was saying— what he would be sacrificing to come to her—if he went through with these plans.

"Yitz'khak, you dare not quit the Yeshiva! You must become a rabbi!

"I can finish Yeshiva in America."

"Yitz'khak, they might not have Yeshiva in America! You must finish Yeshiva! I will not allow you to give up your dream—your calling from Elohim—because of me!"

"Alright, my darling Faygel. I will finish Yeshiva. I will somehow find time to work while I study and while I do my rabbinical duties. Baruch HaShem ... Bless the Lord, He will make a way."

Suddenly he was on his knee in front of her. He took hold of her hand. His dark eyes gazed into hers. "Will you wait for me, Faygel? I don't want any other girl but you."

Her heart pounded inside her chest. "Yes, Yitz'khak. I will wait."

"Even if it takes years?"

"No matter how long it takes, I will wait."

"Promise?"

"I promise. I don't want any other man but you, Yitz'khak." They embraced again both laughing and crying at the same time. Faygala thought Yitz'khak was about to kiss her, but then they heard footsteps in the distance. Quickly they let go of each other and began walking innocently around the barn again. But Faygala's heart was so full it almost hurt.

The day before the departure, Mama said, "Come help me, Faygala. You will need food to take with you tomorrow." They cooked and baked together all day. They made chicken, potato kugel, bopkeh, and several loaves of bread. Mendeleh interrupted his playing outside many times and Feivel his work in the animal shed to come in to snitch the delicious food. Mama's exaggerated fussing and little slaps on their hands didn't deter them at all. Faygala cherished this special time with Mama enhanced by the wonderful fragrances that filled the house. She wanted to keep this memory in her mind forever.

That last night Faygala lay in bed crying out to Elohim the way Yitz'khak said they should, feeling the Spirit of HaShem along with the stove's heat feeding strength and courage into her soul and body. The warmth coursed through her blood filling her with vitality and the resolve to do what she had to do. The words, "With my Shepherd's help, I will be strong" entered her brain and flowed down into her heart. "I will fear no evil." Her inner voice took up the cadence of her pulse and sang her thoughts as she breathed deeply in and out until the words softened to a lullaby. "Mama knows best. I will go and I will wait." She fell asleep clutching the piranee, a memento of her mother's love and a symbol of her future life with Yitz'khak.

"Wake up Faygala, mein shvester, my sister." Little Mendeleh had sneaked out of bed and climbed the rickety-ladder up to the loft. He shook Faygala's shoulder. "Tell me a story." She pulled him up beside her and covered him, snuggling his warm, little body next to hers. She was missing this sweet, little four year-old boy already. "I will tell you how the streets are made of gold in America where I am going and someday soon, you will go, too, Mendeleh." She scratched his back. "He is so small," she thought. "Who will tell him stories? Who will sing to him? Who will teach him to be strong?" This time she didn't tell him one of Papa's stories. This time she made up her own. In soft murmuring tones, she began, "Once there was a fine, big boy, and his name was Mendeleh . . .." As he lay in her arms, she transformed their straggly little hut into a majestic, sparkling manor with waxed, wooden floors here, and soft plushy, red carpets there—carpets that you could lose your toes in when you walked barefoot on them. More beautiful than the Mayor-general's house with its slate tiles; it was a palace with a glass roof that glistened like the icicles that hung from their windows in winter. "Mendeleh, when you look up and see the stars twinkling and shining each night, remember that they are the same stars Papa and I will be looking at so you will never, ever be lonely."

He whispered, "Now tell me about Cleveland, Ohio where you will live and where Papa lives now."

Softly Faygala said, "Our Papa lives in a beautiful, big house in a city where the streets are washed clean every day and all the people are very kind. They get new clothes to wear on Rosh Hashanah, and they have wonderful things to eat—khallah, gefilteh fish, and taiglach smothered in honey. They eat that every day."

"Every day is like Shabbos in Cleveland, Ohio isn't it?" he smiled sleepily. "Yes, and we will send for you and Mama and Feivel soon, soon, soon...." Finally he drifted off to sleep.

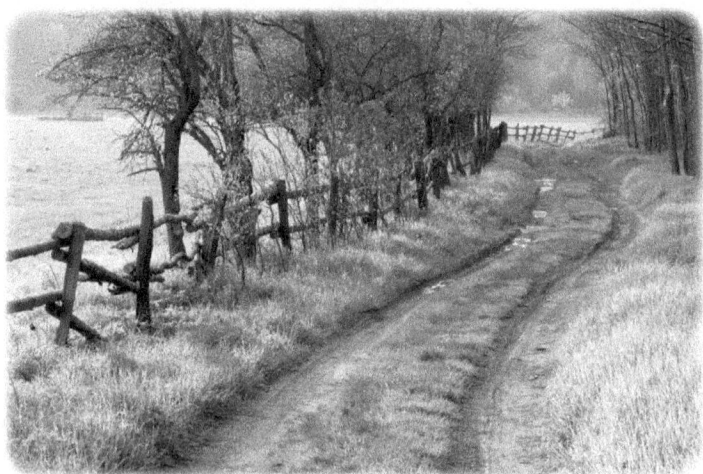

THE WAGON

Too soon, Mama was calling Faygala to get up and get dressed. The sun was just creeping up over the bank of pine trees in the east. Pincus and his family would soon be there with his wagon and horses. No time for a hot bowl of kasha. "Hurry Faygala, I've got the food basket for you. You'll eat your breakfast on the way. Here, take my black shawl. You'll need it to go to Shul on the Shabbos."

"Mama, not your best shawl! What will you wear on Shabbos?"

"Hush, now. You need it. HaShem, bless His Name, will take care of me."

Mist was rising from the ground, and dark clouds hung low on the horizon. Feivel helped Faygala up into the creaky old wagon then handed up her bundle of clothes. Pincus' two little girls, Soreh and Rivkah, huddling together among all the other bulky bundles, moved over to make room for her. Faygala placed her bundle next to them and sat on it. Mama handed up her piranee and the basket of food which was to last until they reached Odessa.

Mendeleh came running out of the house crying. Faygala lay aside the basket and piranee, leaned over the wagon and reached down to him. Feivel lifted him up so Faygala could give him a proper hug. She squeezed him tight, "Be a brave boy and take care of Mama for me. Okay?" He nodded his dear little head as Feivel pulled him away. She sat back down, pulled her heavy black skirt down over her feet and wrapped her piranee around herself over top Mama's special black shawl to keep warm.

The horses stomped their feet and snorted spray into the cold, damp air. Pincus, sitting on the high seat up in front of the wagon was anxious to get going, "Nu cum shain! So, come on already!"

His wife, Gittel, motioned for him to wait. She leaned down from beside her husband to shake hands with Mama, "Zie gezunt ... be well, Rochel, we will take good care of your Faygala."

"Zol dir Gut bentchen ... God bless you, Gittel," Mama answered.

"Be a good girl, say your prayers, and keep the Shabbos," Mama admonished Faygala as she cradled the girl's face. "I love you, mein ziskeit."

At the last moment, Yitz'khak arrived and said a shy good-by. Faygala's heart gave a leap. She felt even more assured of his promise, seeing him be brave enough to declare his love openly in this manner. Mama and Feivel looked a little surprised, but then they smiled. Too soon the horses began clip-clopping down the hard earth road.

Faygala turned and waved to her family and her Yitz'khak until they grew too small to be seen. Then she sank down heavily and wiped away her tears. When would she ever see any of them again? She was now on her way to a new life with a kuzineh she barely knew anymore—only from the few letters Kuzineh Khannah had written over the years—but also a life with Papa, whom she would always know well. She couldn't wait to hear his loving, strong voice again. That hope was what sustained her.

Pincus' horses clopped along the roads past fields and through woods on their way to the seaport. At night they stopped at a shtetle where Jewish families were glad to give them food and a place to sleep. They were happy to help someone escape the troubles of Russia. Each family hoped to be able to leave someday, too.

Some nights there was no shtetle in sight. Then the group slept in the wagon under a huge tarp that Pincus fastened down on the corners. Sometimes they ate while the wagon was moving; sometimes they stopped and had a picnic on the ground on the tarp. When it rained, they held the tarp over their heads as the horses trudged ahead.

Those spring rains soon turned the hard-packed ruts into muddy rivulets. Sometimes the wagon wheels seemed to half disappear in the mud. The girls fell against each other as the wagon lurched and jostled through the mess. Gittel climbed down into the wagon with them to help protect her daughters from falling out. It was only by Pincus' expertise, that they were able to arrive all in one piece in Odessa.

After a few days, the last forest receded and soon they saw that the horizon ahead had turned to a deep blue. The whiff of ocean breezes lifted their spirits and stimulated the horses to pick up their pace. "Oy Pincus!" Gittel grabbed her husband's hand, "We are here! Gut sudahnk ... Thank God!" She turned around in her seat to look at the girls, "Soreh! Rivkah! Faygala! Give a kook ... a look. Can you smell that? That is the ocean. We are here! Gut sudahnk!"

They went directly to the docks, full of ships, looking for theirs. They looked at every ship but didn't find it. Pincus could speak a little Russian in addition to Yiddish, and he asked a policeman where to find their ship. The policeman told him, "It left last week, but another ship will be here next month. Don't worry."

"Nu, vos ken wir tawn ... So, what can we do?" They asked themselves. They had to find a place to live until their ship came. Pincus and Gittel had come prepared with the name and address of a Jewish lady who took in roomers. "We will go look for her; it will be alright," Pincus comforted the girls.

The city was noisy with throngs of people of different nationalities, many also waiting for their ships to come in. Pincus had to maneuver his wagon slowly down the bumpy, muddy streets. Men in harsh, loud voices called out their wares from pushcarts. Ladies in dark, heavy clothing and black, knitted shawls clutched the hands of crying children and bargained shrilly for a bit of this or that from the vendors. Faygala saw some women with painted faces standing in doorways or leaning out of windows and calling to men to come in to see them. She shuddered and wrapped Mama's shawl tighter around herself.

Pincus' horses made their way haltingly through the masses and over the bumps. Faygala had to hold down the little girls who kept jumping up and down with excitement, shouting to each other to look at this side of the street or that side. She was afraid they might fall out when the wagon lurched into the puddles. Gittel hung onto Pincus to keep from being jolted off their high seat.

Faygala's head was in a whirl. She was glad she was not alone in such a wild place. The horses stomped their feet and whinnied their protest at the delays caused by people walking in between the wagons to get to the other side of the street. "Move on!" A policeman shouted to Pincus. This scared the two young girls.

"Oy vay is mir ... Woe is me," Soreh started to cry and Faygala lifted the little one onto her lap.

"I don't feel so good Faygala," Rivkah scooted close and leaned against Faygala, clutching her arm.

The directions, Bless HaShem, were good and Pincus found the rooming house. The lady in charge was a big beefy woman with thick black hair fastened into a bun at the nape of her neck. A heavy man's shirt covered her large bosom and stocky body down to her hips. She had roughened red hands. Her shrewd black eyes looked the group over carefully before taking them in. Her name was Nachomkeh and she had three children.

Five years ago her husband had left for Canada saying he would send for them as soon as he could save enough money for their passage. That was the last she had ever heard from him. A sister in Ottawa wrote that she heard he had married a rich widow in Hamilton. Nachomkeh was resourceful. To support herself and her children, she had convinced a Russian gentleman to let her manage his rooming house. Russian laws forbade Jews from owning property or operating a business, but people sometimes looked the other way if it benefited them.

There was a room on the second floor that Pincus and his family rented. Faygala moved into a little attic room on the third floor. Nachomkeh had a kind heart and she took a liking to Faygala, so she gave her room and board in exchange for Faygala helping in the kitchen and taking care of her children. Furthermore, she watched over the girl and gave her advice just like a mother, "Faygala, be careful when you go out into the street. You should keep your money pinned inside your *untervesh* ... underwear. There are *gonavim* ... thieves here. They will steal everything if they see you look like a greenhorn." Another time she cautioned her, "You should never go out alone. There are men who look for young girls to take them away and do who knows what!"

Faygala didn't need to be told advice like this anymore. She had learned her lesson. In her mind, the dark leering faces of the Cossacks were never far away. She stayed close to the house, never leaving it except to go out shopping for food with the women.

One day Pincus took her to the ship line's office to buy her passage. There had not been time for her to buy it in advance like Pincus had done for his family. After Nachomkeh's talk, she was afraid that someone might steal the "ship's card" they gave her, so she pinned it to the inside of her clothes with the money left over after the purchase. She wore it that way until the ship arrived.

There was one thought in Faygala's mind that made the long wait for the ship seem like a gift. She kept thinking maybe Yitz'khak would have time to come join them. Perhaps he would quit Yeshiva in spite of her protests and find a way to get to Odessa. She didn't want him to do that for his sake, yet she did want him to for her own sake.

Everyday she gazed longingly down the street, hoping to see him coming her way. She scanned her eyes across the passing crowds longing to see his face. Her heart jumped when she saw one that looked like him from a distance, only to be disappointed as he neared. One time she was so sure it was Yitz'khak's back she saw ahead of her. His hair was the same sandy red color. The side curls were tight, but slightly unruly, exactly like Yitz'khak's. Even his sauntered steps were like Yitz'khak's. She almost called out his name, but the young man turned and her heart fell.

After a month of waiting, their ship finally came into the harbor. This caused much excitement in town. Everybody ran this way and that to spread the news. The mood was contagious. Rivkah's and Soreh's giggles and glee could not be calmed down. Faygala couldn't join the joy. Yitz'khak's failure to appear was too disappointing.

Faygala gathered her clothes together, making sure her money and her "ship's card" were pinned safely to her bodice under her heavy woolen blouse. She fell into Nachomkeh's arms crying, kissing, and thanking her for all her kindness. Nachomkeh said she felt like she was losing a daughter and cried with her. Faygala told her, "I will write to you, I promise. I will never forget you. Ich lieb dir ... I love you. Gut zol dir benchen ... God bless you. Look for me in America if you ever come."

Pincus and Gittel had already sold their wagon and horses, so they piled their few belongings into a cart they borrowed from Nachomkeh and pushed it down to the pier. Nachomkeh's nephew came along to bring it back. Faygala followed along, clutching Soreh's and Rivkah's small hands so they wouldn't be run over by horses or wagons or get lost in the mad rush. Faygala couldn't believe how many people there were trying to hurry to the ship. She still searched for her loving rabbi. She wouldn't give up hope until the end. How wonderful it would be to sail with him across the ocean.

She stayed close to Pincus and his family while they waited to board. She clutched her precious "ship's card," her ticket to a new life of freedom now released from her bodice and in her hand.

"Steerage," the officer said when they handed him their tickets. Steerage is deep down in the bowels of the ship near the ship's steering equipment. The immigrants were cargo and they were held in the same kind of space, without portholes or effective ventilation. The passage going down to the compartments at the bottom was dark and steep. Faygala carefully placed her feet on the slippery stairs, clutching her bundle of clothes and her rolled up piranee to her chest while holding onto the damp, narrow iron pipe that served as a handrail. Rivka, right behind Faygala, held onto the rail with one hand while clutching and leaning heavily on Faygala's arm. There was no way to keep their skirts from trailing on the filthy steps. Gittel carried Soreh on one hip with a bundle clutched in one hand and another under the other elbow, while still managing to keep a hand on the rail. Pincus was piled high with the rest of the bundles. He went ahead of them all so as to catch them if they slipped.

Faygala found an empty top bunk in one of the compartments on the women's side. Gittel found another across the aisle from hers. Soreh would sleep with her; Rivkah with Faygala. There were about twelve aisles or hallways of metal bunks, stacked three high, attached to walls on either side.

She decided to use her bundle as a pillow and her piranee as a cushion on the lumpy, dirty mattress, thankful that, it being so warm in the hull, she wouldn't have to use the thin, worn blanket that didn't look clean. She felt sorry for the women heavy with child who would have to sleep on these uncomfortable bunks. Many people had to leave some of their bundles on the floor, and Faygala worried that such a woman would trip over them and have her baby right there.

After arranging their personal items they scooted back up the precarious steps together to stand on deck to watch as the ship moved away from land. Pincus and Gittel lifted their girls up so they could take in the whole exciting view. Loud cheers arose both from the crowd on the ship and from the masses watching from the shore as the sails were hoisted up. They shouted again when the huge sea vessel began pulling away. Faygala and the Pincus family watched their Russia—their homeland—grow smaller and smaller.

THE SHIP

A gain, Faygala scanned the sea of faces on deck for her beloved. She stepped up on the piles of ropes and the short rope-wrapped posts to get a better look. But it was all to no avail. There was no Yitz'khak.

It wasn't long until the joy in the air turned into moans and groans as the ship swayed in the waves. People began moving to the steps, clutching their bellies. Others hung over the railings and vomited into the dark waters. Pincus' girls were among them.

Later in the hull below, Faygala and Gittel tried to comfort the sick little girls while feeling miserable themselves. Faygala heard other children crying and mothers comforting them in an assortment of languages she could not understand. She could make out some Yiddish and German, but the rest seemed to blend into a babble. However, Faygala did recognize the tones and concerns of motherhood that is alike in any language, and she felt a connection with the sisterhood.

Being so low in the belly of the ship, the noise and throttle of the engines and the rocking motion of the ship caused such severe seasickness that many people clung to their bunks the entire three weeks of their ocean trip. Without proper ventilation, babies became quite ill and cried constantly.

This new feeling of seasickness felt horrible to Faygala. Sometimes she didn't think she could make it to the toilet at the other end of the hallway in time. Many children didn't. The awful smell that ensued nearly choked the already suffering passengers. Gittel unwrapped a couple pewter dishes from a bundle to use to catch her girls' vomit. In spite of their own sickness, she and Faygala managed to keep the girls clean and comfortable.

The little Polish girl in the bunk below Faygala, threw up all over her blanket. Faygala, sick as she was, got down from her bunk to help the mother clean up the mess. She got some water and started scrubbing the ragged, dirty, ship blanket. "Gevalt!" Faygala screamed, "Lice are crawling out of the blanket."

There were lice everywhere. People seemed to be scratching their heads all the time. Faygala and Gittel kept theirs and the girls' long hair in braids and carefully fine-combed it every day hoping to keep free from the bugs. That's all they could do. They couldn't bare to bathe or wash their hair in the greasy, grimy toilet rooms and wash basins. Their careful combing efforts didn't work. Soon they were all itching, too.

When Faygala and the girls began feeling better, they went up the stairs to walk on the foredeck. Gittel still felt sick, so Faygala took the girls to give their mother some rest, but Faygala never walked alone with them. She was still afraid of what might happen. She met two girls named Miriam and Chashkee who were about her age, and they walked with her. They were traveling alone. Soon all three became fast friends.

Both girls were Jewish and had experienced hardship in their shtetlach in Lithuania, which was under Russia's control. Miriam told them that last year Cossacks came storming into her shtetl on a Jew-killing spree, a pogrom, at *Pesakh,* Passover. When her mother got word that the Cossacks were on their way, she hid with Miriam and her two younger sisters under the haystack in the barn behind their house. The other villagers took to the woods, so no one was killed, but the drunken soldiers went into their houses, smashed the furniture, and stole anything they could lay their hands on, then burned some of their houses down. Miriam and her mother felt devastated at their loss, but felt blessed that their house wasn't burned.

Each day the three girls walked arm in arm, telling each other more about their families. Rivkah and Soreh held their hands or played around them. Miriam confided that she was worried she wouldn't recognize her father, "I don't even remember my Papa. He is coming to get me in Ellis Island. If I don't recognize him, they will send me back home. He went away when I was only four years old. My youngest sister was only a baby!"

"I will recognize my Papa when he comes to get me. He's only been gone three years," Faygala said. She began telling them how wonderful her father is. She didn't tell them that she actually worried that no one would come to meet her when they docked at Ellis Island. She was afraid there hadn't been enough time for a letter to get to Papa.

If no one came, she would be sent back to Russia, too, and how would she get back to her shtetl? She had been making herself sick thinking about what could happen. She had heard terrible stories about girls vanishing and never being heard of again. She determined not to tell any of those stories to Miriam. It would only frighten her more. Faygala tried hard to keep her own terrifying thoughts away, but horrible pictures kept creeping into her consciousness when she least expected it. Hearing Miriam voice her fears didn't help Faygala. Suddenly Faygala realized that Chashkee was talking about her Papa.

"...left when I was ten." Chashkee said. "He has a good job in a factory where they make men's suits. He sent ship's cards for Moisheh and Yossel, my older brothers a few years ago and they work in the factory too. Papa knew the Russians were taking Jewish boys as young as 15 for their army, so he had worked hard to get the money to send them tickets before the Russians came for them." Chashkee began to cry, "For a Jew to go in the Russian army is death. They took my cousin Shmuel, and no one knows what happened to him. He never came back. *Tahnteh* Leah cries all the time for him."

Suddenly Faygala realized that she should be thankful for the Cossacks. They were keeping the Russian army away from her village! Chashkee dried her eyes on her sleeve and straightened her shoulders, "My brothers sent me my ship's card and they said I can work in the factory, too. Then I will send for my mother and younger brother and sister."

Every day the girls had the deck pretty much to themselves because most of the people were so seasick they hardly left their bunks. The girls were young and strong. Their bodies had adjusted to the movement of the ship better than some of the older folk. They started going to the dining room for meals, where they met some other young people: Hungarian, Polish, Czechoslovakian. Most of them were Jewish, trying to escape persecution. Some Italians came on board when the ship stopped at a port in Sicily.

One Italian boy had carried his accordion with him across the Sicilian Mountains to get to the seaport. Russian Jewish boys taught him to play exciting Jewish music. Even though most of these young people couldn't understand each other, they all joined in the singing and Jewish dancing—girls in their circle on one side of the room; boys on the other. Sometimes the musician played his native Italian songs. They found they could dance their Jewish dances to that music, too.

Younger children like Soreh and Rivkah joined in the fun. Soon adults did, too. Pincus came and danced letting his young daughters come over to the men's side. He would break away from the men's circle and make a new, tiny circle with his daughters. On the very calm days, Gittel was able to dance, too. The little girls ran back and forth between dancing with their father, then with their mother, giggling with delight the whole time. They danced inside the circle of all the women, including Faygala and her friends, trying to copy the dance steps, but failing in a very cute, amusing way. Faygala laughed for the first time since she left home.

Finally the ocean voyage came to an end. When the ship entered the New York Harbor, the immigrants hurried up to the decks. They crowded against the railings for their first sight of the Manhattan skyline. Mothers and fathers held up their children so they could catch a glimpse. A loud shout went up when the Statue of Liberty became visible through the mist, beckoning the immigrants to come taste "life, liberty, and the pursuit of happiness." People of all nationalities jabbered excitedly in their native tongues, clinging to each other and crying from exhaustion and thankfulness. They were at the "Golden Door," the "Island of Hope." Little did they know that some of them would find out why it is also called "The Island of Tears."

The ship docked near the welcoming statue. An immense spread of red brick buildings stood on the other side of the Hudson River, with the New Jersey docks in the background. The island lying so low in the water, made the buildings look like they were rising up out of the sea instead of sitting on land. But the spiraling towers on each of the four corners of the main building filled Faygala with dread, because it reminded her of the strange, foreboding churches in that awful port city of Odessa. The long history of persecution by the church made any Jewish person of her day shudder at the sight of a cathedral type building.

She, her two friends, and the Pincus family ran

downstairs to get their possessions. Carrying her bundle of clothes and piranee, with Rivkah in tow, she struggled up the stairs, hardly able to see over the top of her heavy load. Her arms ached, but she couldn't put the load down for fear of losing it in the pressing crowd of people waiting to get off the ship and to board the barge that would carry them across the expanse of water to Ellis Island.

While they were on deck, Rivkah chose to hang onto her father's arm instead of onto Faygala's. She had missed her father a lot on the ship. Then in the mad rush, Faygala somehow got separated from the Pincus family. A lump of pain grew in her throat. She felt very alone. Would she be able to find them again? Would the little girls get lost without her to help watch them? If they didn't find each other at Ellis Island, would they ever see each other again? She was sorry she hadn't gotten the address of where they were going.

Faygala didn't see Miriam or Chashkee either. She tried to look for them, but people were pushing and shoving. She was unable to fight the crowd.

As she stepped off the gangplank, the ground felt wobbly under her feet. She didn't have time to get used to land because she was pushed directly onto the waiting barge. The barge was not big enough to carry all the passengers from the ship. Others had to wait for the next barge. Once on board, Faygala looked again for the others, but to no avail. She gave up and just stood at the railing watching her future come into view.

When the barge moored at the dock on Ellis Island, policemen barred the immigrants from disembarking. The exhausted travelers, some dressed in their native costumes for this special occasion, were made to wait another two hours until those ahead of them were finished being processed. Faygala didn't know what was happening. The fear of being sent back welled up in her again. Some women began to cry and their men tried to push the policemen out of the way.

When they were finally able to leave the barge, officials wearing uniforms met them and placed identification cards around the immigrants' necks, stating their ship's name and the immigrant's number from the ship's master list. The uniforms frightened Faygala because she thought they were soldiers like the Cossacks. She didn't know why she was pushed into a circle with some other people—herded like sheep. She stood there trembling as she waited. No one knew what was going to happen to them.

She felt safer when a man, who was not wearing a uniform, came to their circle to explain the inspection. He spoke in Yiddish and Polish and said that there were other men who could speak Italian and some of the other languages.

He took them to the basement of the main building to a door marked "Baggage Room" in several languages and directed them to leave their bundles there. Faygala saw piles of piranees and trunks and bundles lying around on the floor. She hoped her belongings would still be there when she came looking for them.

The Yiddish-speaking man led her "group" up a long, wide stairway. Men in white jackets stood on both sides of the stairs watching the people as they climbed the marble steps. Faygala stopped to help an old man who was limping. Then she noticed one of those white-coated men looking at her from higher up the stairs. He wrote down something on the paper he held in his hand. When she and the elderly man and his wife reached that inspector, he put a blue chalk mark on the old man's back and sent him to a room. The old man's wife started crying and yelling, so they let her go with him. The stairs led to a huge, open, great hall with balconies all around and a very high ceiling. Faygala got dizzy looking up at the ceiling, it was so high.

Uniformed men were shouting, "Hurry along! Go! Go!" They herded people into different lines. One line led to a serious-looking, wrinkled-brow, white-coat wearing doctor who took a buttonhook and flipped up Faygala's eyelid to look in her eye. She gave out a yell, and her eye smarted and teared. It hurt for two weeks afterwards. "No trachoma," the doctor said and passed her on to the next line where another doctor pounded her back and listened with something in his ears. When they passed her along into a room with other women, she had to take off her blouse. Even though it was a woman who listened to her chest, Faygala was very embarrassed. She was mortified when she saw children staring at her. The children's mothers kindly looked away. In this room also, everyone's head was treated for lice.

When she got through with all the lines, Faygala had to go to another room where an immigration officer sitting behind a desk asked her some questions. She didn't know what he was saying, so another man who spoke Yiddish, had to come in to explain. Faygala turned around to take out her $25 hidden in her bodice to show the men that she had money and "was not destitute." In Yiddish, she told them her Papa was coming to get her and that she was going to live in her cousin's house and work as a maid for the family. All the time she talked, she bent her head and looked down at her lap. The men kept shouting in Yiddish and in English, "Speak up! Speak up! We can't hear you." The immigration officer behind the desk wrote down something on the paper in front of him, and the man who spoke Yiddish told her she passed the test and that "Fannie" was her American name now, Fannie Naganov.

Faygala was shocked. Why were they taking her name away? She wasn't sure she wanted an American name. She liked the name Mama and Papa had lovingly given her. "Fannie" sounded very strange to her. It wasn't even close to sounding like her real name.

Then she remembered what Papa had written to them. When he had come to Ellis Island three years ago, he didn't understand English at all and had answered "Naganovitzki," thinking the inspectors wanted to know where he came from. "That's too long for a last name," an immigration inspector had said and wrote down Naganov in the appropriate blank on Papa's form.

"Ah zay gait ... That's the way it goes in America," Papa wrote to Mama. "In the shtetl, everybody knows who I am. Rabbi David doesn't need a last name to call me to the Torah. He gives a geshriye ... a yell, 'Yakov ben Abbe ha-Levi,' and I know he means me. It's different in America." An immigration inspector gave him a new American first name, too. Papa wrote Mama to send his mail to Mr. Jacob Naganov, because that's how the mailman will find him in Cleveland, Ohio.

In the same way, Faygala became Fannie Naganov. The harried immigration inspector expediently filled in the blanks on Faygala's registration form in front of him, and she started her Americanization process. Remembering Papa's easy-going attitude, taking it all in stride and even seeing humor in it, she tried to be more like him. "Fannie Naganov, Fannie Naganov," she kept repeating her new names to herself, trying to get used to them.

Faygala walked out of the room in a daze, unsure what to do next. To her delight, she spotted Miriam and Chashkee standing in the hallway. The three embraced each other. "Oy Faygala," sobbed Miriam. "Chashkee told me a doctor put a blue chalk mark on my back." She turned around so Faygala could see it. "I coughed while they were examining me. I couldn't help it! Now I have to stay here in their hospital for more tests to make sure I don't have tuberculosis. If I do, they will send me home"

The girls clung to each other and cried with her. "Elohim willing, you will pass the tests. Try hard not to cough when they are checking you!" Faygala tried to sound hopeful. "You will get better and we will see each other again. Remember, I am going to live with my kusineh in Cleveland, Ohio. You must try to come visit me."

"How will my papa find me now?" Miriam cried. "He is coming for me, but he won't know where I am!!" Miriam was whisked off to the hospital. The two girls could hear her pitiful wails all the way down the corridor as the nurse hurried her away.

Chashkee had a sty on her eye and the doctors gave her something to heal it. Thankfully, she did not have to stay in the hospital. Their fathers would be coming the next day to pick them up. Faygala and Chashkee were taken to the women's dormitory on the second floor to stay the night. A matron came to take their clothes away to be deloused before they were given cots to sleep on.

Later that night, the two girls walked around on the balcony overlooking the main floor, savoring their friendship and vowing never to forget one another. All was quiet downstairs, for everything had stopped promptly at 5:00, to be continued the next day. Other immigrants, not yet tested, were fed in the dining room and sent to other dormitories for the night.

"Will we ever see each other again?" Faygala wondered out loud.

Immigrants just arrived from Foreign Countries—Immigrant Building
Ellis Island, New York Harbor. Copyright 1904 by Underwood & Underwood

...dway, New York's Great Commercial...
Copyrighted 1904 by W...

THE CITY

Chashkee told Faygala she was going to live with her father and brothers in New York City. "Papa wrote that it is on the East side. That should be easy enough to find," Chashkee assured her. Neither girl had any idea how huge of a city, New York was.

"My Papa wrote us that Cleveland is somewhere in the middle of America. So, you should be able to find me, too," Faygala felt reassured. Both girls were unaware of the expansive size of their new country.

The next morning when Chashkee's Papa arrived, the girls threw their arms around each other, tears flowing freely down their faces. They were each other's last vestiges of familiarity.

Faygala was sad saying good-bye to her friend, but she looked forward to seeing her Papa. She was not sorry to see the last of Ellis Island. She wanted to breathe fresh air and see grass and trees. She was tired of being pushed around and told what to do and when to do it. But most of all, she was tired of crowds of people and the noise. She needed peace and quiet.

Faygala was expecting Papa to come to get her, but no Papa appeared. In spite of her efforts to calm herself, the things she had worried about the whole time she was on the ship now haunted her again. Was it really going to happen? Was no one coming to meet her? Would she be sent all alone back to Russia? She would never be able to get all the way back home without the Cossacks finding her again! She fought back tears as she frantically continued searching the crowds, looking for Papa.

Suddenly her eye was drawn to a slender, confident-looking lady coming her way from the other side of the great hall. The lady had a fur piece wrapped around her neck and a stylish, red feather stuck right in the middle of her soft black hat. Faygala wasn't sure why she was paying any attention to this lady. She didn't look Jewish. She didn't dress like the married women at home who covered themselves with long sleeves and high-necked dresses. She didn't have her hair wrapped in a marriage scarf as the women in Naganovitzki do. Faygala had heard there were some Jewish ladies in the big cities like Warsaw, Poland who called themselves the "Moderns." Perhaps there were "Modern" Jewish ladies here in America, too.

The lady was walking straight towards Faygala and as she got closer, Faygala saw that she looked like Mama!

She was about the same height and had the same olive coloring and dark brown eyes that sparkled with life and warmth. (Bubbie Etkie had told her that when Mama and Kusineh Khannah were young girls, people said they looked like twins.) This lady was Kusineh Khannah! She looked like a "Modern," slender version of Mama!

Faygala was immediately swept up in an explosion of emotion with hugs and kisses and tears. "Oy Faygala, Faygala, how beautiful you are! You look like your mother!" Kuzineh Khannah exclaimed.

Faygala cried with happiness and relief, "Kuzineh Khannah, Mama said you are an angel, and tahkie ... surely you are my angel." Faygala held on to her and did not want to let go. "At last, at last," she sighed, "at last!"

Her cousin extricated herself and gently corrected Faygala, "Hattie, my name in America is Hattie. Mrs. Hattie Cohen.

"Hattie?" The name felt awkward on Faygala's tongue. She didn't like calling her beloved kuzineh by this new, foreign name. She didn't know if she could make the switch in her mind.

"What's your American name? They gave you a new name, too, didn't they?" Kuzineh Khannah asked.

"Fannie," Faygala said sheepishly. "Fannie Naganov."

"Good. At least they got it right in giving you your papa's last name." Kuzineh Khannah pronounced.

Faygala started realizing that her kuzineh was right. Although she would always be Faygala in her heart and to Mama, having the same last name as Papa will be very nice. It connected her even more with him. It gave her more of a sense of family and security. "Family is so important in America that they give you all the same last name," Faygala would later write her mother. "Ah zay gayt in America." She was learning to be more like Papa.

Kuzineh Khannah proceeded to vouch for "Fannie" to the authorities that "Fannie" would not be a burden on the United States government. "Fannie" would be living with her and working as a maid for the family. Faygala looked on in amazement, listening to Kuzineh Khannah speak so clearly and directly to the immigration officers. She saw that her cousin was not afraid to speak to men and she didn't lower her eyes. "How different American women are from Yiddisheh," she thought. But as soon as they were away from Ellis Island, Kuzineh Khannah lapsed easily into comfortable, singsong Yiddish, washing away the strain of the long ocean voyage for Faygala and cementing their relationship with more love.

Kuzineh Khannah led Faygala to the Baggage Room to retrieve her bundle of clothing and her piranee. Yes, it was there. It had not been stolen! Then they joined the long line waiting for the ferry to take them to Manhattan. When it came, they boarded it and stood at the railing, Kuzineh Khannah's arm protectively around Faygala's shoulder, both women marveling at the New York skyline.

Before returning to Ohio, Kuzineh Khannah had promised her older brother, Khaim, they would stop overnight to see him and his family in Brooklyn.

"I love New York!" Kuzineh Khannah told Faygala. "Yankel and I come as often as we can to visit my mishpokha ... family."

The tall buildings dazzled Faygala. They seemed to touch the sky. Kuzineh Khannah pulled her back from the street center rail, just in time, as a streetcar went whizzing by. "Watch out, Faygala! You must pay attention!" Kuzineh Khannah ordered caringly.

Faygala had never seen a street car before. She was shaken. New York was too fast-moving and scary! She hung close beside Kuzineh Khannah, one arm hugging her bundle of clothes to her chest; the other hand clutching her Kuzineh's coat sleeve, as they dodged people right and left. Suddenly everyone stopped as a very loud thing came speeding towards them. People jumped out of the way as it sped by. Faygala screamed with fear.

"What was that?!" Faygala asked.

"I don't know. I've never seen anything like it." Kuzineh Khannah answered. "Maybe it is a street car gone off its tracks. It was a very strange looking street car though. And it didn't have its wires." The whole crowd around them was exclaiming about it in English, which Faygala could not understand.

"I've never heard anything so loud!!" She said to Kuzineh Khannah.

"Me either. My ears feel numb. Let's hope we never see anything like that again!"

They continued on down the street. A steady stream of horse and buggies and horses and wagons filled the street. Horse manure was everywhere. Faygala noticed one horse and wagon going slowly by as men behind it hurriedly shoveled up the manure. But it was obvious that no matter how fast they worked, they could never keep up. In Odessa, they could easily keep up, because there were more people than animals on the streets there.

"Ooooh, what is that smell?" Faygala cried out as a horse pulling a barrel kind of wagon went by very close. Faygala was used to the smell of horse manure and to the smell of the public toilet buildings they had passed. Outhouses were a fact of life in Faygala's day, but this smell was ten times worse.

"Oh, they are carrying the stuff from the cesspools to dump it in a pit out in the country."

"What's a cesspool?"

"Oh, that's where the stuff goes from the public toilets. It's a big pit under the building. When it gets full, they have to empty it."

"Oh, my! What an awful job!"

"Somebody's got to do it," Kuzineh Khannah said casually. She led Faygala to a door on the sidewalk where a throng of people were entering. "Be careful going down the stairs, Faygala,"

"Where are we going?"

"To get on the train underneath the street."

"There's a train under the street?!"

"Yes, it's a new thing! It's called the 'subway.'" Kuzineh Khannah guided her down the steep stairs and dropped two nickels into the turnstile at the entrance to the underground world that opened up before them and the train huffing and puffing and screeching to a stop. They ran to get on the waiting train with the sign "Flatbush" on it. Faygala was speechless and Kuzineh Khannah pushed her into the first empty seat she saw. Kuzineh Khannah stood over her, hanging on to the overhead strap, hugging Faygala's precious piranee with her free arm.

"Oy vay iz mir," Faygala gasped, trying to catch her breath.

Kuzineh Khannah laughed, "Welcome to America, Faygala, I mean Fannie."

"I could not believe the different kinds of very fast trains in New York," Faygala would write to her mother later. "One goes down the middle of the street and another goes under the ground." There were a lot of other things she would experience for the first time in America. They got off at their stop, barely escaping the doors that slammed shut behind them. They climbed up the flight of stairs into the emerging sunshine, which blinded Faygala at first. She was relieved to find the street much quieter here.

Khaim had a little hole-in-the-wall tailor shop around the corner. His wife Celia was with him and they welcomed the two travelers with loud cries of joy. "So, this is the maidel we've all been waiting for," Khaim exclaimed.

"Tahkie Hattie, she looks like you. What a beauty!" At first Faygala wondered who Khaim was talking to—who was Hattie? Then she remembered. Kuzineh Khannah is now Kuzineh Hattie.

Celia held out her arms and embraced Faygala, "Oy, what a long trip for a young girl to take alone! Cum Shain, we'll go home now. Khaim, you'll close the store. Today is yontif, a holiday. Baruch HaShem! Faygala got here safe."

Their warmth enveloped Faygala and swept away the confusion and fear that had been with her ever since she had left her home in the shtetl. She followed along docilely, still clutching her bundle of clothes, while Khaim and Celia led the way to their apartment house down Albany Avenue, talking excitedly with Kuzineh Khannah, exchanging news about their families. Faygala was surprised when they stopped in front of the big brownstone building that Khaim said was his home. She couldn't believe people lived in such a big place. Up three flights of stairs the little party went, stopping to catch their breath at each landing, inching their way toward the open door of apartment number 301 where the rest of the family impatiently awaited the new arrivals. "They're here! Here they come! I hear them coming up the stairs!" Laughter and accented voices drifted down the stairwell to welcome them.

A throng of aunts, uncles, and cousins descended upon them, embracing Faygala and Kuzineh Khannah before they reached the upper landing, eager to help with their baggage. Celia let all the relatives know that Faygala was in the United States, and Kuzineh Khannah was bringing her here before going home. They came bearing gifts for Faygala and all kinds of delicacies for the table. A holiday mood was in the air, and one of the cousins started to sing in Yiddish, "Tzu Mir Hoss Gacummen a Kuzineh ... To my house comes a cousin" to the accompaniment of spirited clapping.

Before the meal, the ladies quickly whisked Faygala's piranee, Mama's shawl, and a bundle of clothes to the back room and began scrubbing them. They wanted her to be free of lice. They chatted excitedly while they worked. They treated her hair again, had her bathe herself, and don a new dress—one of the gifts given her.

They all gathered around a very long table that filled the parlor. Children ate in the kitchen. How everyone fit into that small apartment was a wonder to Faygala. She tried to remember who was who by where they were around the table, so she could write about the evening later to her mother. They were all Mama's cousins—people Faygala had known her whole life from Mama's stories about them all growing up together in Naganovitzki. Now, she could put faces to the names in those stories. In no time at all, Faygala's heart was knit with theirs.

An even livelier conversation ensued when Kuzineh Khannah mentioned the noisy, runaway streetcar. "It's not a street car. It's a new contraption that runs by itself, no wire, no rails, no horse, just a deafeningly loud motor," Kuzin Khaim explained. All the women were shocked that such a thing existed. All the men had strong opinions about this new invention.

"It is too dangerous for the city."

"Don't worry. It's just a fad. It won't last long."

"Yea, it's too expensive and not near as reliable as a horse, I hear."

"Just a toy for the rich to show off."

"Well, I think they need to be outlawed before people on the street get hurt."

By ten o'clock, everybody had said their goodbyes, and Faygala and Kuzineh Khannah were glad to drop into bed in the living room on what Celia called her "sofa bed." Lumps and all, the weary two slept through the night and were awakened by the smell of coffee and the sounds of Celia opening and closing cupboard doors in the kitchen, putting dishes on the table for breakfast. By the early hour of five o'clock, they were heading out the door, well fed with a box filled with more of Celia's bagels, *lax* (pickled salmon), and cream cheese. Khaim took the morning off to take them into the city on the trolley to get to the railroad station in time for their eight o'clock departure.

Saying goodbye to him and Celia was hard, "Come visit us soon, we'll have a picnic," Kuzineh Khannah said as she kissed her brother and sister-in-law.

"Goodbye, thank you. I'll write to Mama, how nice you all are," Faygala said in Yiddish and retrieved her bundle of freshly washed clothes and the new suitcase filled with more clothes her relatives had given her. Kuzin Khaim carried the other packages of gifts she had been showered with. Kuzineh Khannah was waiting on the steps with Faygala's precious piranee.

THE TRAIN

New York Grand Central Train Station was a huge, vaulted cavern of a building. It looked like the inside of a castle to Faygala with its shiny, towering, brick walls and high ceilings. Faygala's ears rang from the loud announcements of train schedules bouncing off the walls all around, back and forth, back and forth. The sea of people raised their voices to be heard over the waves of echoes. The place was even noisier than Ellis Island had been. When the approaching trains blew their whistles, Faygala nearly screamed at the unbearably, deafening sound. She wanted to cover her ears but couldn't because of her full hands.

She was very relieved to finally get inside the train where the noise level was much more tolerable. She and Kuzineh Khannah felt blessed to get two seats together in the nearly packed full, coach car. They gratefully set their burdens down and sank into the firm, overstuffed cushions. Resting their feet on their bundles and boxes, they were glad to settle in for the long trip to Cleveland. Faygala heaved a sigh of relief, "Oy, is gut to have rest and quiet."

"Zer gut ... Very good!" Kuzineh Khannah took off her hat and coat, laid them carefully beside her, unfolded the piranee, spread it over the two travelers, leaned her head back, and promptly fell asleep. Faygala was left alone in her thoughts.

It was cool in the train. The pre-dawn, late spring coolness still hung in the air which became fresher and cooler as they left the smelly city. Faygala took in a deep breath of the clean, freshness, pulled Mama's shawl close and snuggled with the piranee, thankful for the warmth and reminiscence of home. The enthusiastic, welcoming embrace of the Brooklyn relatives and listening to them speak in Yiddish had revived her. Since leaving home, there had been very few people she could understand.

On the ship the converging voices of Italians, Poles, Greeks and other immigrants blended into a cacophony that rivaled the churning of the ship's engines. It was even hard for her to understand the different dialects of Yiddish, although, if she concentrated, she could usually figure out most of what was being said. And since Yiddish borrows words from several other languages, she was often able to piece together an idea of what people of other languages were talking about. But English was too hard to understand because she had nothing to relate to it. It sounded like total jibberish to her.

Faygala shuddered reliving the helplessness she felt when it was her turn to face those scowling immigration inspectors on Ellis Island and the white-jacketed doctors who poked and prodded. She hadn't been able to understand them or get any idea what they wanted from her. She had never felt so alone and miserable in her life.

But now the cloud of confusion and depression lifted. She was here in America. She was safe sitting next to Kuzineh Khannah, who seemed to radiate comfort and security.

"This train is going so fast, it looks like the whole world is flying by," Faygala murmured under her breath in Yiddish. She looked out the window at the large, green yards, nicely sprouting vegetable gardens, and neatly painted houses in the small shtetlach as they went speeding by. "In America, everything is different!" She shook her head in amazement and shrugged her shoulders. The worn high-backed plush seat in their compartment comforted her as she leaned back and closed her eyes; the tightness in the back of her neck easing up a bit.

Her dozing Americanized cousin, curled up beside her, stirred and opened her eyes. She reached over and took Faygala's hand, "Faygala darling, you don't have to be afraid any more," her soft voice reassured Faygala. It warmed her heart that Kuzineh Khannah forgot to use her American name. "Here in America is different."

Faygala nodded, "Everything is different here, Kuzineh Khannah."

"Hattie, my name in America is Hattie. And "kuzineh" is "cousin" in English." As she watched her beautiful cousin yawn and slip back into dreamland, Faygala forced herself to try harder at thinking of Kuzineh Khannah as "Cousin Hattie" now.

Later, Cousin Hattie stirred awake again and began reminiscing, "Faygel, I know how hard it was for you to say goodbye to your Mama and everybody. I was only two years older than you are now when I married Yankel and we left to live in America. I had to leave everybody, too. We came with nothing, and we went to live with Yankel's older brother Shimmon in Cleveland, Ohio. He owns a window and glass business there. Shimmon showed Yankel the business. My Yankel is a fast learner, praise be to Adonai, and now he's a partner with Shimmon."

Faygala was impressed, "Only in America! Tahkie ... Surely, the streets must be paved in gold in Cleveland."

Cousin Hattie was wide-awake now and she wanted to talk, but Faygala's eyes kept drooping, she was so tired. Cousin Hattie's voice droned on and on, with Faygala catching a word here and there. It was a long train ride and Faygala kept drifting in and out of sleep. She was dreaming she was walking down the golden streets of Cleveland, Ohio with Cousin Hattie and Rabbi David's youngest son, Yankel.

Faygala woke up feeling too warm. Cousin Hattie opened her eyes. She had given up on talking to Faygala and fell asleep again. Now she sat up, folded up the pi-ranee and set it aside. "Fannie, we should be home by tomorrow morning." She found her big paisley handbag hidden under the pile on the floor and carefully took out an envelope she had put in the side pocket for safe keeping. "Look Faygala, here are pictures of Yankel and our children. This is Rebecca. She's five years old. Little Esther here was just two years old last month," she said, her eyes glistening with pride, "and our twins, Joey and Morty are studying for their bar-mitzvah." Cousin Hattie was so engrossed in talking about her beloved children that she didn't realize she had slipped back into using Faygala's Russian name. "Faygala, you'll see how much our little girls and boys are anxious to meet you." She clapped her hand to her forehead, "Oy, boys, what am I saying? Soon they will be men! Before you know it, they'll be wearing long pants. They grow up so fast. Darling, you will be like a big sister to them and a daughter to me," Cousin Hattie fondly squeezed Faygala's hand.

Now, with both of them wide awake, the two cousins chatted away. Hattie laughed at Faygala's shy questioning of her boldness with the authorities, and told her that women in America were being educated, too. Her neighbor's daughter, Rosalie even started to go to college. "Faygala, American women want to vote just like their husbands. It's a lebedikka velt ... a wonderful world! Just think, Faygala, maybe in a few years, when you are a citizen, you will be able to help pick out our president, just like Yankel and Shimmon."

The train was chugging along. Faygala wriggled into a more comfortable position and listened contentedly to the stories her cousin was telling her about the family and relatives. The Cohen's live in a big brick house with dark green shutters, an upstairs, a downstairs, a cellar, and four big bedrooms. "Gevalt!" Faygala could hardly believe her ears. It seemed like her cousins lived like the czar. They had a wrap-around porch where everyone would sit in the summer evenings because it was so hot. In the big back yard, there were two sour cherry trees, an apple tree, and a little Seckel pear tree. An arbor stood far back loaded with grapes that Yankel would use to make his own wine for Pesakh. Inside the house they have a big kitchen and a toilet upstairs.

Faygala sat bolt upright in her seat. "You mean it is inside the house?" She shook her head. She couldn't believe it! She hated going to the outhouse in the middle of the night. It was always dark and, in the winter, it was freezing. "It's going to be a pleasure living here in America. I'll be like a princess," she exclaimed.

"And in the same room, hot and cold water comes out of pipes from the wall, so you can take a vanee ... a bath too."

"What? Water coming out of the wall? You mean you don't have to carry the water into the house in buckets?"

"No! And we don't have to pump it either. It takes no work at all to get the water to start flowing. There are two water tanks in the attic. The hot one siphons hot water from the tub on the boiler in the basement. We don't use the hot water much in the summer; mostly in the winter. We also have gas lights on the wall that are lit by gas pipes also coming through the walls."

"What is 'gas'?"

"It's a special kind of air that comes through the pipes that burns much brighter than kerosene."

Cleveland, Ohio was sounding better and better! "I'm going to have so much to write home to Mama." And to write to Yitz'khak, she added in her thoughts.

Cousin Hattie patted Faygala's hand as she painted her bright, American future for her. Her caring voice had a lulling effect on Faygala, "You'll help me with the housework and with the children. And when you're ready, you can go to Night School just like I did. You'll learn English so you can become an American citizen. You'll make new friends...." Faygala snuggled down into her seat and covered herself with Mama's shawl again. She felt chilly again, but not cold enough to need the piranee. She closed her eyes, giving in to the drowsiness that engulfed her, and she fell asleep again as the train winded its way toward Cleveland, Ohio.

The train's clickity clack, clickity clack that had lulled Faygala to sleep, now brought her back to wakefulness. She sat up in her seat to peer out the window at the passing lush landscape. Her eyes opened wide as they took in the big farmhouses and fields, bigger than any she had ever seen. "There must be many rich people here in America," she marveled. Cousin Hattie looked up from the book she was reading. "This is rich soil and these people are farmers. They own their own land. We have no peasants in America, Faygala. I mean Fannie. They grow wheat and those tall stalks are corn."

They were now in Ohio and they would soon be home, Cousin Hattie told her. "Your Papa will meet us at the train station. He didn't come to Ellis Island because he doesn't have his citizenship yet and his English still isn't too good. Yankel and Shimmon have to take care of the business, so it seemed better I should travel the 800 miles to New York City to get you."

Faygala was interested in the shtetlach they passed through. In her mind the small towns were villages. "Look Cousin Hattie." She was learning to use the correct name. "The train tracks run right through the middle of the shtetlach here. I remember when Tahnte Khayeh wanted to go to Kiev, Zaydee ... Grandfather had to borrow Pincus' wagon and horses to take her way out in the middle of nowhere to wait for the train to come, and then they had to flag it down and hope it would stop."

Cousin Hattie nodded, "I know. I remember how it was in Russia. We have a beautiful train station here in Cleveland. Of course, it is not as big as the one in New York City, but it is very modern."

The conductor came down the aisle calling, "Next stop Youngstown, Ohio. We'll be there in 15 minutes." Cousin Hattie stood up and stretched to her full height of four feet, 10 inches. "Faygala, we have to change trains in Youngstown, then we'll ride straight through to Cleveland." She checked the delicate little gold watch, hanging on a thin gold chain around her neck. "Let me see, it's 11:30, so we can *chahp a nahsh* ... have a snack here in this city. We don't have to get our train until 4:30 this afternoon. It will be good to walk around outside and get some fresh air." Faygala gathered her bundles together and followed her cousin off the train.

Cousin Hattie checked their baggage into four lockers, and they walked outside to get their bearings. Faygala expected to see the streets crowded with people like in New York City. She was pleasantly surprised to see just two or three people walking along the street, and a few one-horse buggies waiting for customers in front of the railroad station. Cousin Hattie waved the drivers away when they approached her. "Come Fannie, it is good to stretch our legs after such a long trip."

Faygala had only been in two big cities in her life, New York City in America and Odessa in Russia. In both places, she had been afraid to walk alone. She clutched her cousin's arm, remembering warnings given her. Cousin Hattie gingerly extricated herself, "Faygala, it's all right, you don't have to be afraid anymore." (Cousin Hattie had forgotten the American name again, which made Faygala smile inside.) "Youngstown is not like Odessa or even like New York City. It's safe here."

New York and Odessa were different from anything Faygala had ever seen in her lifetime. "I will never forget the noise and smells and crowds of people there. It is such a relief to walk here without bumping into somebody or have somebody bumping into me," she told Cousin Hattie. "I hope Cleveland, Ohio is like here." She started to enjoy herself and realized that she was hungry. Cousin Hattie steered her across the street to a little restaurant that looked inviting.

"Fannie, there are not so many Jewish people in Ohio like in New York, so I don't think we can find a kosher restaurant. We will go in here and have some milchik ... milk, a piece of bopkeh, called pie in English, and coffee. We'll eat later when we get home."

Faygala found the pie very interesting. "So much fruit! It's very different from bopkeh!" Feeling refreshed, after *chahping a nahsh*, they walked along the sidewalks, breathing in the fresh air and peering into various shops. A train whistle split the quiet of the afternoon. Faygala grabbed Hattie's arm, pulling her back toward the station. "We're going to miss our train!"

"Faygala, it is too early for our train," Hattie calmed her. "There are many trains that come into this station. We have plenty of time yet."

Soon a small stream of people exited the railroad station. Faygala watched with interest from the distance. A few got into the waiting buggies, and the horses went clip-clopping down the brick street. A young family came out and the little boys started running around chasing each other, yelling at the top of their lungs.

"Is different in America," mused Faygala. "Children run wild here, ah zay vee *vilda chaiyas* ... like wild animals!"

"Everything is different in America," Cousin Hattie agreed.

By three o'clock that afternoon, Hattie was ready to go back to the depot. With all the walking they had done in New York, her fragile dress shoes had caused a blister on her foot. She needed to sit down. "Oy, Faygala," she said. "Is nisht goot, ir toot mir vay ... It's not good, it hurts me."

Faygala looked down at her own sturdy, worn shoes. "Americanized women are not so strong as women in der haim ... at home," she thought.

Back on the train, Faygala's thoughts began to wander again. The past three months were a jumble of memories. Half of the time she didn't know where she was. Sometimes when Faygala closed her eyes, she was right back in Russia in her little shtetl with Mama, Feivel, little Mendeleh and her beloved Yitz'khak. Physically, this train was taking Faygala to the end of her journey, but mentally, she was miles away across the ocean, just starting out on that gray, dismal morning in April. The clip-clopping of all the horses on the street of Youngstown had reminded her of Pincus' horses clopping along the roads on their way to the seaport.

The swaying motion of the train as it chugged along lulled Faygala into a fitful sleep. She awoke to a gentle tugging on her arm and the soft, sweet voice of her cousin, "Fannie, we're here. You're home."

The conductor came down the aisle calling in a loud voice, "Next stop Cleveland, Ohio. Have your tickets ready." He helped Faygala collect her bundle of clothes, the suitcase and boxes of gifts her relatives had given her in Brooklyn. Cousin Hattie carried one box and the bulky, treasured pirannee that would be a comfort to Faygala for years to come, reminding her of der haim and of Yitz'khak.

Papa and the whole Cohen family were waiting to greet her. They converged on her in a single unit with Papa at the head. "Faygala, Faygala," he clasped Faygala to him. He repeated over and over, laughing and crying at the same time, "Gut sudahnk, Gut sudahnk. Baruch HaShem. Baruch HaShem." Suddenly he stopped. "Is this your Mama's Shabbos shawl?"

"Yes, Papa."

"I thought so. The special shawl I bought for her. And it still has the smell of her in it!"

Faygala took the shawl off and reverently handed it to him. "Here, Papa," she said. He took it and buried his face in it, bobbing his head and twirling around with it the way someone might move to lessen the severity of bodily pain.

"Oh, Rochel, how I miss you." Faygala heard his muffled voice say into the shawl. The whole group of people kind of froze at seeing Papa act this way. They quickly looked away out of politeness, as if the moment was too private to be observing. When Papa handed the shawl back to Faygala, there were tears spilling down his cheeks. Faygala gave him another hug letting her own tears flow freely. Papa patted her shoulder to comfort her.

As Faygala was wiping her eyes with Papa's handkerchief, she found herself engulfed in another bear hug from the big, bronze-skinned, giant of a man who was Rabbi David's youngest son, Yankel, Cousin Hattie's husband. "Aw, little kuzineh, now is not the time to cry. Now is the time to rejoice! You are in rich America, the Promised Land! And you are with a huge mishpokha who loves you!" His jolly mood soon had Faygala smiling again. The twin boys, taking on the role of being almost men, bravely and solemnly stepped forward to properly greet her, but the little girls shyly hung back behind their father.

"This is your cousin, Fannie," Cousin Hattie told her children. Still the little girls hung back.

"She is not Fannie to me," Papa declared, smiling, as he put his arms around Faygala again. "She will always be mein Faygala," he said in Yiddish, then added in his heavily accented English, "my leetel bird."

Another crowd who had politely hung back for these initial greetings, now approached. The whole extended family, the mispochah, had turned out to welcome Faygala along with landsmen folks from Naganovitzki shtetl. Everyone was talking and laughing at once as they vied for position next to Faygala to hug and kiss her. Uncles, aunts, and old neighbors asked in Yiddish for news of brothers and sisters they had left in the shtetl years ago.

They were eager to hear any bit of information Faygala could tell them about der haim, their home. "Ah vee gait mein brudder Pincus un di shviggerin, Gittel ... How is my brother, Pincus, and sister-in-law, Gittel?," a spritely matron asked.

"Pincus and Gittel?! You know them?" Faygala was happy to hear their names! Then to her great relief, she learned that she would soon see them and their dear girls again. They were living with Gittel's relatives in New York, but planned to eventually move to Cleveland, too!!

A young man stepped forward to embrace her, "Faygel, do you remember me? I used to teach you the *aleph-bayz* ... alphabet when I would come home from the Yeshiva to visit my father. Remember how you wanted to go to school, too"

"Hershel!" Faygala let out a yell. "I am so glad to see you. I didn't recognize you. You don't have a beard any more, and you are so tall and brown." Hershel was Pincus' son from his first marriage and had left Naganovitzki when his mother had died and Pincus had remarried. Faygala had thought Hershel was much older because he was always so serious, but here he was now, young-looking with a big smile on his face and his eyes sparkling with happiness. It actually made him look kind of handsome. She noticed that besides his beard, his side curls were also gone. This concerned her, but she decided to wait until another time to ask about it.

"I am working in the business with Yankel and Shimmon, so I will see you later," he told her as he relinquished his turn with her to another neighbor.

Her relatives' voices and laughter rose to marvelous heights and warmed the air with their unabashed exuberance. Their gaiety enveloped Faygala and lifted her spirits in spite of her exhaustion. She was drawn into their circle of love and acceptance. It was a circle that happily widened to embrace her with a promise of security and happiness.

When Papa noticed the piranee, he clapped his hands and sang out, "Faygala, zol bald zein ah kaleh moid ... will soon be a bride." He took her arm and danced around with her like he did when she was little. "Mein taiereh, claineh maidel ... My dear, little girl. How I wish your mama were here!"

"I wish Mama were here, too," she told him and wiped her eyes again with his handkerchief.

"In time, in time, we will all be together," he promised her.

Faygala kissed him, "Ich lieb dir, Papa." Then she kissed Cousin Hattie and hugged her, "Ich lieb dir aichet ... also. I will always remember the ziskeit ... sweetness of this family, my mishpokha."

Cousin Hattie took Papa's handkerchief and blew her nose and wiped her eyes, "You know. I miss your Mama, too," she said to Faygala. "With Adonai's help, we'll get her and Feivel and Mendeleh here soon."

And Yitz'khak, thought Faygala. This reunion would be so much sweeter if he were here to enjoy it with me. Her heart ached thinking how long it will be before she sees him again, if ever. But I will wait as I promised—even if it does take forever. Her heart began to shed tears at that painful thought. But on the outside she forced a smile.

Papa drew near Faygala and discreetly placed a note into her hand, then winked at her and patted her hand as if to say, You will want to read this in secret. Faygala carefully slipped it into her pocket. Her thoughts went wild trying to figure out what in the world could be in that note!!

"Nu cum shain ... So, come already!" Cousin Shimmon was anxious to get back to his business. "I have to get back to close down for the night. We'll have plenty of time to celebrate later."

Yankel started shooing everybody toward the exit. He picked up Faygala's suitcase, "Come Faygala, let's go home now," he said. Faygala beamed and walked beside Yankel, the now braver little girls joined on either side of her, grabbing her hands. Papa and the twins followed, carrying Faygala's boxes of gifts.

Cousin Hattie moved to the front and turned to face the whole bunch. "Faygala's new name is Fannie. She is in America now. We all need to start calling her Fannie, except for you, Jacob."

Hershel picked up Fannie's piranee. Cousin Yankel led the procession out of the building. "Fannie," he said, "welcome to America."

That night in her new, private, gas lamp lit bedroom lying on the softest bed she could imagine, Faygala opened the note. When she saw who it was from, she sat straight up and could hardly stifle her squeal of delight.

THE LETTER

Naganovitzki, Russia
May 3, 1904

My Beloved Faygel,

Baruch HaShem, Adonai has provided! I listened to you and have continued my studies. I am almost finished. I told my father about my desire to work to make money to go to America. He said he has been planning on sending me because it is getting more and more dangerous for young men here. He has already saved a lot of money for my passage. He has also contacted people in America and found that many communities are in need of rabbis because they do not have a Yeshiva set up yet. One large community in Rochester, New York wants me to come there. They are sending the rest of the money I need! Isn't it wonderful to trust in Adonai?

I will come to Cleveland first to fetch my bride. I have received a letter from your papa giving me his permission to take you as my wife.

I miss you so much. The long wait is almost unbearable.

Your Yitz'khak

Faygala could not believe what she was reading! Nor could she contain her joy! She was going to see Yitz'khak again! Tears of relief filled her eyes. Reveling in the miracle of being with Papa again and of Yitz'khak being able to come, she cried half sobs, half giggles of joy. Finally, she sat at her new desk and looking through her happy tears, she first wrote a quick, joyful letter to Mama.

Cleveland Ohio
June 6 1904

Dear Mama

Baruch HaShem I have arrived safely in Cleveland And Yitz'khak is coming soon too!! Can you believe it!! We are going to get married!!

You were right I am going to like it here I am going to start Night School after Rosh Hashanah I will study hard so I can get a job and save my money to help Papa bring you and Feivel and Mendeleh to Cleveland Ohio too You must come in time so we can prepare for my wedding together!

America is different but mishbocha is the same here just like in Naganovitzki I will tell you more in my next letter Everybody sends their regards to all of you Zei gezunt Ich lieb dir

Your Faygala — Fannie

After finishing this note, Faygala proceeded to write a long, detailed letter of love to her beloved rabbi, telling him all about her adventures coming to America and describing what a promised land it is.

GLOSSARY
OF THE
YIDDISH WORDS

AI - AY   as in may (maidel)
EI - EYE as in eye (Feivel)
EIN - INE as in wine (zein, mein)
KH or CH - (no English equivilant) a
    hard "h" or soft "k" (Khannah)

ADONAI   the LORD
AH ZAY GAIT   so it goes
ALEPH-BAYZ alphabet [aleph (a) - bet (b) in Hebrew]
BAR-MITZVAH ceremony celebrating a boy becoming
    a man at age 13
BOKHER   student. Also means "young man"
BUBBIE   grandma
CH is pronounced like KH, like a hard, gutteral H
COSSACKS   special soldiers of the Russian czar who
    were of foreign origin
DER HAIM   the home
ELOHIM   God (in Hebrew)
FAYGEL   bird, the Yiddish name for the main char-
    acter (also spelled fagel, faigel, or feygel)

FAYGALA   little bird, a term of endearment (also spelled fagela, faigele, faigela, feygele or feygeleh); See videos of this word used in Yiddish folk song: http://olivepressbooks.net/faygala-yiddish-refugee.html

GAY GEZUNTEH HAIT go in good health

GEFILTE FISH a type of fish

GESHRIYE a yell

GEVALT   term of exclamation

GEMULTIKHEIT friendliness

GLEZELEH   a little glass [of]

GOLDA MEDINA the golden dream

GONAVIM thieves

GUT NACHT good night

GUT SUDANK thank "good' (meaning "Thank God")

HaSHEM   The Name (in Hebrew) (used instead of pronouncing the Holy Name of God)

ICH LIEB DIR I love you

KALEH MOID bride

KH is pronounced like a hard, gutteral H or soft K

KHAHP AH NASH get a little something to eat

KHAIM life (usually spelled "chaim." Rhymes with "chime")

KHALLAH egg and yeast special Sabbath bread

KHANNAH Hannah in Hebrew

KHOOMASH the Old Testament

KHUPAH   A tallith draped over poles to form a canopy over the bride and groom.

KLEINEH little

KOOK   look

KOSHER   fit to eat according to the Jewish laws of diet

KREPLACH   meat filled dumplings

KUCHEN cake

KUZINEH / KUZIN cousin (feminine, masculine)

LANDSMEN, LANDSLEIT people from the homeland

LATKES   potato pancakes

LAX   lox, pickled, cold-smoked salmon fillets

LEBBEDIKKA VELT   lively or wonderful world

LOKSHEN KUGEL noodle pudding

MEIN ZISKEIT my sweet one or my sweetheart

MEIN SHVESTER my sister

MEIN TAIEREH KIND my dear child

MILCHICK milk

MINYAN   quorum of ten men (required to hold a synagogue service)

MISHPOKHA family

NU CUM SHAIN so come already

NU VOS KEN MIR TAWN so, what can we do

PESAKH   Jewish holiday of Passover

PIRANEE   a comforter usually filled with goose feathers

POGROM Mob attack, condoned by authorities, against persons and property of a religious, racial, or national minority. The term (coming from the Russian term meaning "riot") is usually applied to attacks on Jews in Russia in the late 19th and early 20th centuries. After the assassination of Tsar Alexander II (1881), false rumors associating Jews with murder aroused Russian mobs in more than 200 cities and towns to attack Jews and destroy their property. Mob attacks diminished in the 1890s, but they again became common in 1903–06. Although the government did not organize pogroms, its anti-Semitic policy (1881–1917) and reluctance to stop the attacks led many anti-Semites to believe that their violence was legitimate. Pogroms also occurred in Poland and in Germany during Adolf Hitler's regime. From: http://encyclopedia2.thefreedictionary.com/Pogrom

PUTTER KUCHEN   butter coffee cake

ROSH HASHANAH   Jewish New Year

SHABBOS   Sabbath (Shabbat in Hebrew)

SHAH, SHAH   shhhh, shhhh

SHAINA MAIDEL pretty girl

SHLOFF GEZUNTAHATE   sleep well

SHTETL   village or little town

SHTETLACH villages (plural of shtetl) (See CH)

SHTICKEL little piece

SHUL   synagogue, Jewish house of prayer

SIDDUR   prayer book of Hebrew Scripture prayers

STEERAGE section of the ship for people paying the
              lowest fares

TAHKIE   surely

TAIGLACH little dough, a sweet pastry baked for
              holidays

TALLITH   prayer shawl (pronounced "tahlis" in
              Yiddish, "tahleet" - spelled tallit - in
              Hebrew)

THE OLD COUNTRY   Europe

TOKHTER daughter

TORAH   the first five books of Moses

UNTERVESH underwear

Yeshiva   Hebrew school for studying Torah

Yeshiva BOKHAR   student in the Hebrew school
                studying to be a rabbi

YIDDISH   a language that is a mixture of a few
                languages, mainly German and Hebrew.

YIDDISHEH Jewish women

YIDDISHKEIT Yiddish life

YITZ'KHAK Isaac

ZAYDEE   grandfather

ZISGEIT   sweetheart or sweetness

ZIE GEZUNT stay well

ZITZIT   fringes attached to a tallit and to special
                Jewish undershirts worn by men and boys
                in obedience to Numbers 15:37-41

ZOL DIR GUT BENCHEN   God bless you

ZOL ZEIN SHTARK be strong

EPILOGUE

Rochester, NY
August 20, 2004

My dear Fannie,

I am the child of immigrants, brought up on the rich stories of Yiddishkeit, often sitting at your kitchen table, sipping a glezeleh tea and munching on a shtickel putter kuchen. It was to your home that many of my relatives came, when they sought refuge in America, the "golda medina."

I want to thank you for your courage and fortitude in leaving all that you held dear and going out into the unknown to forge a new life. My heartfelt thanks for giving me your youngest son in marriage. I never had the honor of thanking you personally, because you died when we were still too young to know love. He was just 13. I was only 10. However, I did get to thank your wonderful husband, Isaac. My parents, Hershel and Chashkee, called him "gentle Rabbi Yitz'khak."

You raised four fine, handsome sons and endowed them with your love of Adonai, Torah study, family, education, and hard work. Your daughters are like sisters to me.

I have always felt you and I were kindred spirits. I want you to know I imparted your values to your grand-children, and they in turn to your great-grandchildren. Your "gemultichkeit" lives on in them today. There is a rabbi or pastor in each bunch—all ministering for the Messiah Yeshua, or Jesus as they call Him in English.

Yes! We discovered that the Messiah already came as the suffering servant, exactly as declared in Isaiah 53. But, of course, you didn't read that chapter be-cause it is skipped in the Siddur. O how sweet it is to know Him. I thank your generation for coming to America because we most likely would not have found out about Him in Russia. The Bolsheviks started taking over after you left and Communism was established not many years later.

So again, I cannot thank you enough.

Your loving daughter-in-law,
Bailkee (Betty)

THIS BOOK IS AVAILABLE AT:

olivepresspublisher.com
amazon.com
barnesandnoble.com
christianbook.com
and other websites

BOOK STORE MANAGERS may obtain this book
at wholesale, returnable through

Ingram Book Company

or

Spring Arbor

or through

Olive Press Publisher

by e-mailing: olivepressbooks@gmail.com

THE E-BOOK IS AVAILABLE
on Kindle at
amazon.com

9 780979 087394